GW01606198

Published by Grolier Books, a division of Grolier Enterprises Inc.

Disney Presents The Wonderful World of Knowledge
ISBN 0-7172-8929-X
Dance, Drama and Music ISBN 0-7172-8942-7

First published in 1999

Printed and bound in China by
Toppan Printing Company

Originated in Italy by Articolor

Designed and compiled by
Marshall Editions Developments Limited

GROLIER
BOOKS

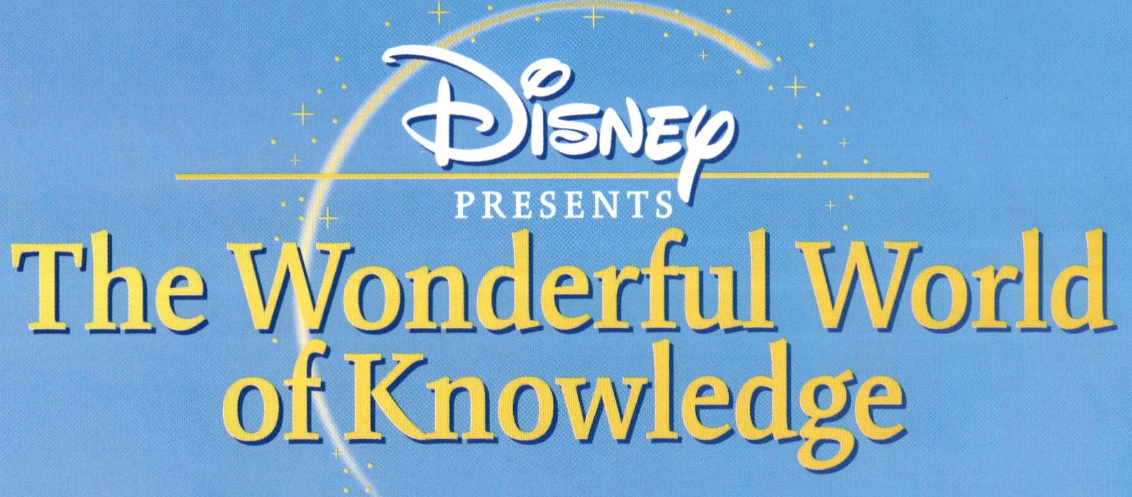

DANCE, DRAMA AND MUSIC

Using The Wonderful World of Knowledge

Mickey, Minnie, Donald, Daisy, Goofy, and Pluto are ready to take you on an adventure ride through the world of learning. Discover the secrets of science, nature, our world, the past, and much more. Climb aboard and enjoy the ride.

Look here for a general summary of the theme

Labels tell *you what's happening in the pictures*

The pictures by *themselves can tell you a lot, even before you read a word*

Mickey's ears *lead you to one of the main topics*

Watch out for special pages where Mickey takes a close look at some key ideas

The Solar System

The Solar System is the name given to our Sun and its family of planets. It also includes the planets' moons, millions of pieces of rock called asteroids and meteoroids, and frozen lumps of dust and gas called comets. Everything else you can see in the sky is outside the Solar System and is far, far away. Every single star is itself a sun, and each may have its own family of planets and moons.

Saturn is surrounded *by beautiful rings*

REPTILES AND AMPHIBIANS

Color and Camouflage

Frogs and toads come in nearly every imaginable color, even gold or black. They have a wide range of patterns, from spots and stripes to zigzags.

Color and pattern help frogs and toads survive. Bright colors warn that they may be poisonous. Drab colors camouflage them, or hide them against their background. Many tree frogs are exactly the same green as leaves, while others look like bark. The Asian horned toad has the best camouflage of all. Folds of patchy, brown skin and a flat body make it look like a dead leaf when it lies still on the forest floor.

Folds of brown skin *give perfect camouflage*

Flat body is hard *to see among dead leaves*

Asian horned toad

False-eyed frog

Markings *look like eyes*

For extra *protection, bad-smelling liquid oozes out around false eyes*

FALSE-EYED FROG

The South American false-eyed frog has large markings on its flanks that look like eyes. These fool some predators into thinking that they are looking at a much larger animal, such as a cat or bird.

COLOR AND CAMOUFLAGE

Dog sniffing *curiously at the toad*

Oriental fire-bellied toad defending itself against a dog

Skin oozes *a stinging fluid*

Bright *colored belly*

Green and *black back*

Toad rears up *on its back legs*

Strawberry arrow frog

POISON-DART FROGS

Deadly poison oozes from the skin of Central and South American poison-dart frogs. People in the rain forest rub the tips of their arrows and blowpipe darts on the skin of these frogs to collect the poison to use for hunting.

Blue poison-dart frog

FIRE-BELLIED TOAD

When cornered by a predator, the Oriental fire-bellied toad of eastern Asia arches its back and rears up on its legs to show its fiery underside. Wise attackers back off, because the toad's skin oozes a stinging, bad-tasting fluid.

FIND OUT MORE
MAMMALS: Camouflage
PLANET EARTH: Forests

16 17

Mickey's page *numbers help you look things up. Don't forget there's a glossary and index at the back of each book*

Goofy and his *friends know how to give you a chuckle on every topic*

Mickey points you to more information in other books in your *The Wonderful World of Knowledge*

FIND OUT MORE
MAMMALS: Camouflage
PLANET EARTH: Forests

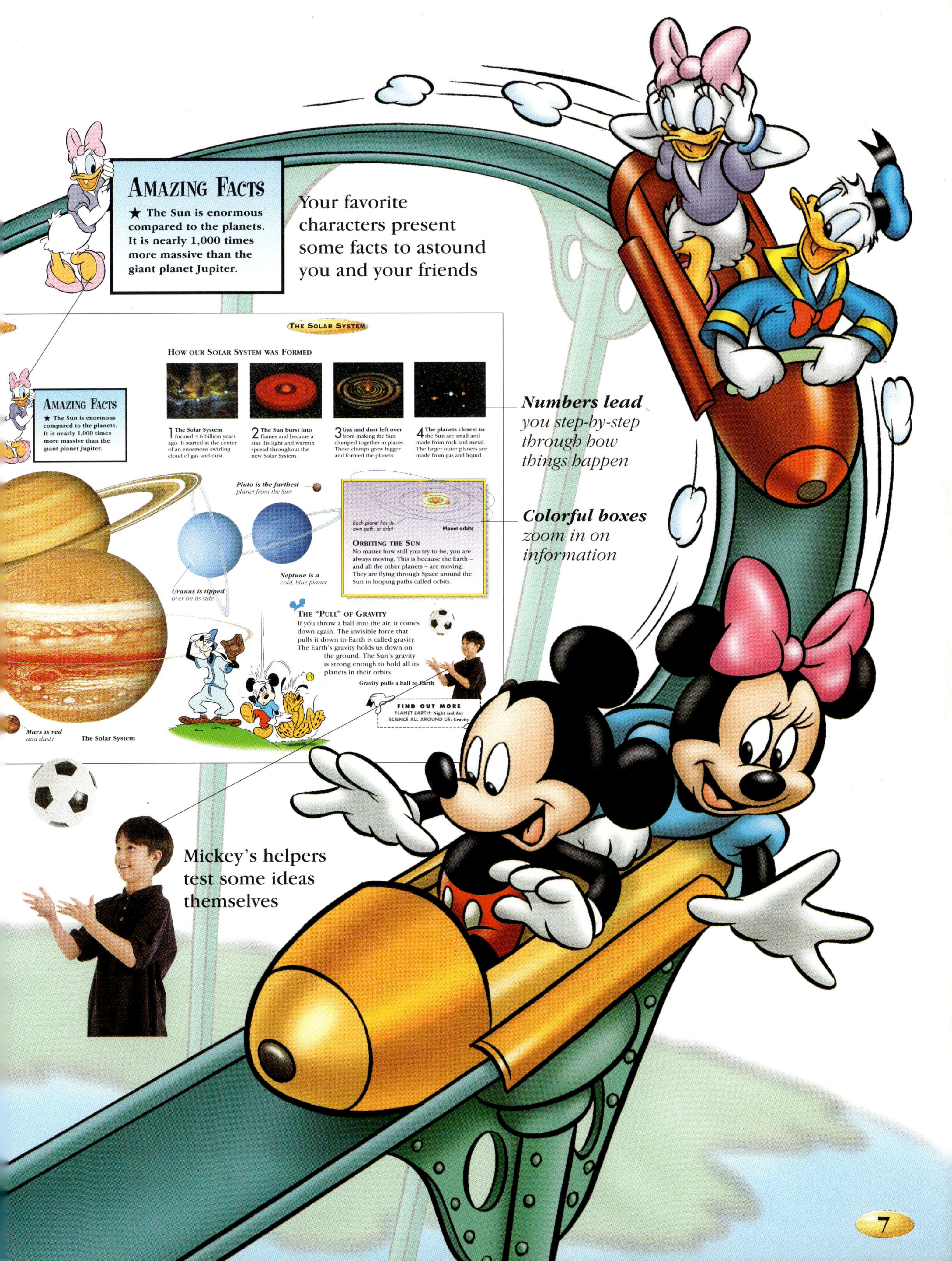

AMAZING FACTS
★ The Sun is enormous compared to the planets. It is nearly 1,000 times more massive than the giant planet Jupiter.
Your favorite characters present some facts to astound you and your friends
THE SOLAR SYSTEM
HOW OUR SOLAR SYSTEM WAS FORMED
1 The Solar System formed 4.6 billion years ago. It started at the center of an enormous swirling cloud of gas and dust.
2 The Sun burst into flames and became a star. Its light and warmth spread throughout the new Solar System.
3 Gas and dust left over from making the Sun clumped together in places. These clumps grew bigger and formed the planets.
4 The planets closest to the Sun are small and made from rock and metal. The larger outer planets are made from gas and liquid.
Numbers lead you step-by-step through how things happen
AMAZING FACTS
★ The Sun is enormous compared to the planets. It is nearly 1,000 times more massive than the giant planet Jupiter.
Pluto is the farthest planet from the Sun
Each planet has its own path, or orbit
Planet orbits
ORBITING THE SUN
No matter how still you try to be, you are always moving. This is because the Earth – and all the other planets – are moving. They are flying through Space around the Sun in looping paths called orbits.
Colorful boxes zoom in on information
Uranus is tipped over on its side
Neptune is a cold, blue planet
THE "PULL" OF GRAVITY
If you throw a ball into the air, it comes down again. The invisible force that pulls it down to Earth is called gravity. The Earth's gravity holds us down on the ground. The Sun's gravity is strong enough to hold all its planets in their orbits.
Gravity pulls a ball to Earth
FIND OUT MORE
PLANET EARTH: Night and day
SCIENCE ALL AROUND US: Gravity
Mars is red and dusty
The Solar System
Mickey's helpers test some ideas themselves

Contents

INTRODUCING

Dance, Drama, and Music

People have always enjoyed making music, acting out true and fantastic stories, dancing, and singing. Today's pop music, with its glamor, rhythms, and quick beat, is just the latest way we have found to express ourselves.

In many lands, styles of performing have not changed for hundreds of years. Some began with serious purposes, such as praising a god or praying for rain. Today, these performances are just as exciting and entertaining as they were long ago.

The Story of Dance

People have always danced. In ancient times people danced and sang to praise their gods or to celebrate big events such as a successful hunt or harvest. Dance is still an important part of many cultures, but today people all over the world enjoy dancing just for fun. Some dances have special steps, which need to be learned. Others, such as disco, let the dancers move freely.

FOLK DANCE

European folk dances used to be part of seasonal or religious festivals and were danced by the ordinary working people. Now these dances remind people of their country's heritage. Many of them are danced in groups.

East European folk dancers

Dancers wear long *headdresses and necklaces of beads*

Dancer from the Tutsi tribe of central Africa

Dancers stamp *their feet*

DRUM BEAT DANCE

In many parts of Africa, dances are performed to the sound of drums. They are danced to celebrate harvests or to welcome important guests. The dancers are usually men.

AMAZING FACTS

★ **The *tarantella,* a dance from Italy, was originally performed as a method of curing the bite of the tarantula spider.**

WAR DANCE

The Maori were the first people to settle in New Zealand. They perform a special war dance, called a *haka*, in which the "warriors" chant, stamp their feet, and make frightening faces to show how strong they are.

The New Zealand rugby team has adopted the *haka* and performs it before each match

Traditional *costumes are often worn*

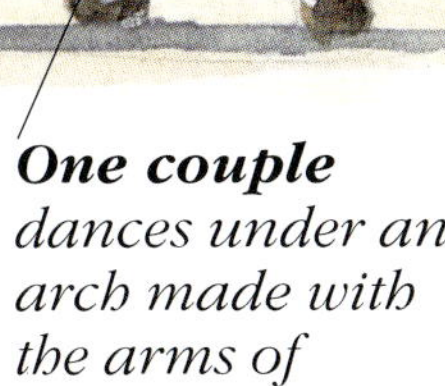

One couple *dances under an arch made with the arms of another couple*

There are no set steps in disco dancing – you move to the music in any way you want

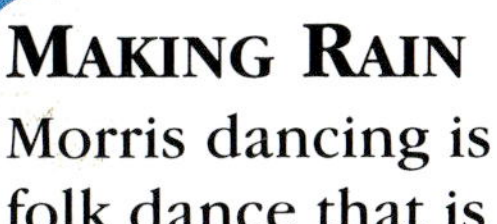

MAKING RAIN

Morris dancing is an English folk dance that is often danced at village celebrations. Hundreds of years ago, the Morris dance was performed in spring to encourage rain to fall to make crops grow.

Dancers knock *their sticks together*

Morris dancers

FIND OUT MORE
CHILDREN OF THE WORLD: Zulu dances
PAINTING AND SCULPTURE: Shiva

Dance-dramas

Dancing and acting are often closely linked, and many dances tell stories. For example, in India some dances tell ancient stories from the Hindu faith. Group dances that tell a dramatic story are called dance-dramas. Dancers act out the story to singing and music using dance and mime. Mime is a type of acting that uses facial expressions and body movements instead of words to describe actions or feelings.

AMAZING FACTS

★ A Bharat Nhatyam performance can last up to four hours – a long time for one performer.

TEMPLE DANCE

Bharat Nhatyam is an ancient Hindu temple dance. It comes from India and is usually performed by a single dancer. Like other classical Indian dances, it uses specific expressions and hand gestures, each of which has a particular meaning.

***Elaborate** headdresses often include gold and precious stones*

***Costumes are made** from beautifully embroidered materials*

Khon dancers in Thailand

***These hand** gestures mean "woman peeping from behind a curtain or veil"*

Woman performing Bharat Nhatyam

KHON DANCERS

The Khon is a dance-drama from Thailand. Traditionally, some of the performers wear masks. They dance and mime to the chanted words of a storyteller. Musicians play during the show, too. The Khon was probably first performed for the king of Thailand nearly 500 years ago.

ABORIGINAL DANCE

The Aboriginal people have lived in Australia for thousands of years. During this time they have created many dance-dramas as part of important ceremonies. Children learn the dances from their elders.

Aborigines paint their bodies for their dances

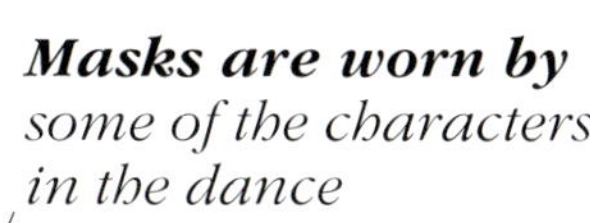

Masks are worn by *some of the characters in the dance*

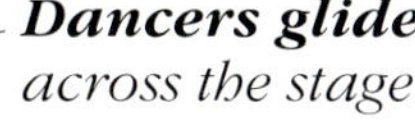

Dancers glide *across the stage*

Dancers move their *feet slowly and carefully*

MARCEL MARCEAU

People who perform mime shows are called mime artists. Marcel Marceau is one of the best-known modern mime artists. He comes from France and is famous for his white-faced character called Bip.

Marceau miming as his character Bip

FIND OUT MORE
CHILDREN OF THE WORLD: Aborigines
COMMUNICATIONS: Body language

Kathakali

Kathakali is a spectacular dance-drama from southern India. It dates back to the 1500s and is still popular today. During the plays, singers tell stories from Hindu legends, while dancers act them out using their special dance language. Kathakali plays are traditionally shown at night in a temple courtyard, and all the parts are played by men.

AMAZING FACTS

★ Kathakali dancers need to have great control over the muscles in their faces. Some masters of the dance have such good control, they can laugh with just one side of the face.

Gold, jewels, and *embroidery decorate the heavy wooden headdress*

An eggplant seed is *placed under each eyelid to turn the eyes red*

Red eyes draw *attention to the dancer's facial expressions*

DAZZLING COSTUMES

Kathakali dancers wear full skirts and layers of jackets. Each jacket is split down the back so the hot dancers can be fanned with cool air between dances. The splits cannot be seen because the dancers always face the audience when they dance.

False nails make *the hand movements easier to see*

Kathakali dancers

Ankle bells *draw attention to foot movements*

TIME TO PREPARE

Preparations for a show can take hours. First, the dancers paint their faces. A make-up artist then adds more detail by sticking layers of rice paper onto the dancer's face. Finally, a tall headdress is tied firmly onto the dancer's head.

Delicate rice paper mask is stuck on with thick rice paste

Each headdress is built on a wooden frame

COLORFUL CHARACTERS

Kathakali dancers wear thick make-up that looks like a mask. The colors and patterns of the make-up have special meanings. Green means goodness, red means bravery and fierceness, black means evil and wildness, and white means purity.

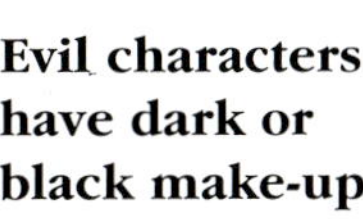

Evil characters have dark or black make-up

Monkey is an important Kathakali character. He is powerful and strong

Female characters have pinkish-yellow make-up for their faces

HAND GESTURES

Kathakali dancers use hundreds of different hand positions, each with a different meaning. Silver false nails are worn on one hand to help draw attention to these gestures.

Tripataka can represent objects such as a crown, a tree, or a lamp

Bhramara shows a bee, a wing, or a bird

Padmakosa can mean a lotus flower or a pot

FIND OUT MORE
COMMUNICATIONS: Sign language
TRAVELERS AND EXPLORERS: Monkey

Ballet

Ballet is a mixture of graceful dancing, beautiful music, costumes, mime, and scenery. Ballet began more than 400 years ago in Europe. At first it included singing and speech as well as dance, and the performers wore high heels. Then, about 200 years ago, ballet dancers began to wear the soft, flat toe shoes they use today.

FIVE POSITIONS

Nearly all ballet steps start and finish with one of five body positions. These were first written down by Pierre Beauchamps, a French choreographer. A choreographer is someone who creates a ballet or dance performance by working out the steps and movements in time to the music.

LOVING A SWAN

In the famous ballet *Swan Lake*, a prince falls in love with a girl who has been turned into a swan. One night the prince is tricked into marrying another girl. Later, he and his swan princess drown themselves in a lake so they can be together.

Scene from *Swan Lake*

Amazing Facts

★ **In *Swan Lake*, the lead ballerina performs 32 full turns without stopping. She balances on one leg and whips the other leg around her body.**

Ballet on Film

Sometimes a ballet is made for the movies instead of a theater stage. In a film ballet called *The Tales of Beatrix Potter*, the dancers wear huge masks to make them look like mice, frogs, and piglets.

Mr. Jeremy Fisher, a character from *The Tales of Beatrix Potter*

Modern dance uses a freer style of dance than classical ballet

Modern Dance

In the early 1900s, some dancers rejected traditional ballet and started a less formal kind of dance known as modern dance. Instead of telling a story, modern dance often tries to express a mood, feeling, or idea.

Toe shoes

Ribbons tied at the *ankles help keep the toe shoes on the foot*

Stiffened toes

Bodies kept still while *dancers stretch out their arms and legs in elegant poses*

Dancers must *be fit and have strong muscles*

Toe shoes *made of satin*

Dancing on Tiptoes

Women ballet dancers are called ballerinas. They wear satin shoes, called toe shoes, which have the toes stiffened with glue. This means the ballerina can dance *en pointe*, or on the tips of her toes, without hurting her feet.

FIND OUT MORE
CHILDREN OF THE WORLD: Ballet school
GREAT LIVES: Beatrix Potter

Ballroom Dancing

Ballroom dancing is usually performed by couples, with the man and woman holding each other as they move to the music. Dances can be energetic with fast steps, or slow with graceful steps. Nearly all of the ballroom dances seen today were developed during the 1800s and 1900s. At first they were danced at parties and public gatherings. Now they are also danced in competitions.

Woman is led by *the man as they move around the ballroom*

Man's left hand *holds his partner's right hand*

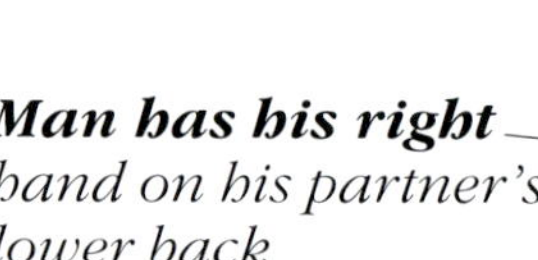

Man has his right *hand on his partner's lower back*

Waltzing couple

Diagram showing where the man's feet should step for the waltz

Left foot

Right foot

DANCING FEET

Books about ballroom dancing often have drawings to show dancers where their left and right feet should step as they turn their bodies. The man's and woman's steps are shown separately, to make things less confusing.

WHIRLING AND TWIRLING

The waltz is an elegant, circling dance from Austria. It became popular during the 1800s. When it first appeared, people were shocked to see a man and woman dancing together so closely.

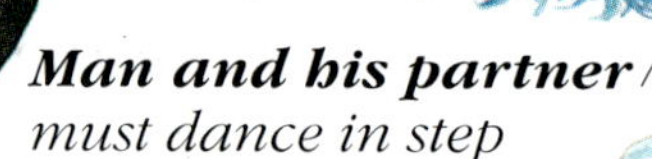

Man and his partner *must dance in step with each other*

STEPPING OUT

The tango is a dance full of slow, gliding steps and sudden stops. It originally came from the slums of Buenos Aires, Argentina, where it was danced by men. Today it is one of many South American dances popular around the world.

Dramatic moves *are an essential part of the tango*

Dancing the tango

Bullfighter whirling his cape in front of the bull

Dancing the *paso doble*

FIGHTING DANCE

The *paso doble* is a Spanish dance in which the man's movements copy those of a bullfighter in a bullring. The woman represents the cape the bullfighter holds in the ring.

AMAZING FACTS

★ **The inventor of roller skates, James L. Plymton, decided to show off his new invention by skating around a ballroom while playing a violin. But he could not stop and crashed into a mirror at the end of the room.**

BALLROOMS

Up until the 1940s, grand dancing parties, called balls, were very popular. They were held regularly in huge ballrooms. Some ballrooms had mirrors around the sides so the dancers could watch themselves as they danced.

Ballrooms were elegant places, where many people enjoyed dancing together

Each step must be *as smooth as possible*

FIND OUT MORE
ATLAS OF THE WORLD: Flamenco
COMMUNICATIONS: Symbols

Puppets and Puppet Shows

Puppet shows have been performed since ancient times – the remains of puppets have been found in the tombs of Ancient India, Egypt, and Greece. Puppets were often used to act out legends or religious stories.

Different types of puppets are operated in different ways. A glove puppet is worn on the hand, while a rod puppet is worked by sticks held from below. A marionette, or string puppet, is worked by moving a wooden cross to which the puppet's strings are fixed.

Playing with different types of puppets

Rod puppet

Marionette, *or string puppet*

Glove puppet *with hand inside*

As many as 50 *puppets can appear in a Wayang Kulit show*

Wayang Kulit show in Indonesia

SHADOW PUPPETS

In Wayang Kulit puppet shows, the puppets are held behind a thin screen and a light casts the puppets' shadows onto the screen. Women in the audience sit in front of the screen, watching the shadows. Men sit behind the screen and watch the puppets themselves.

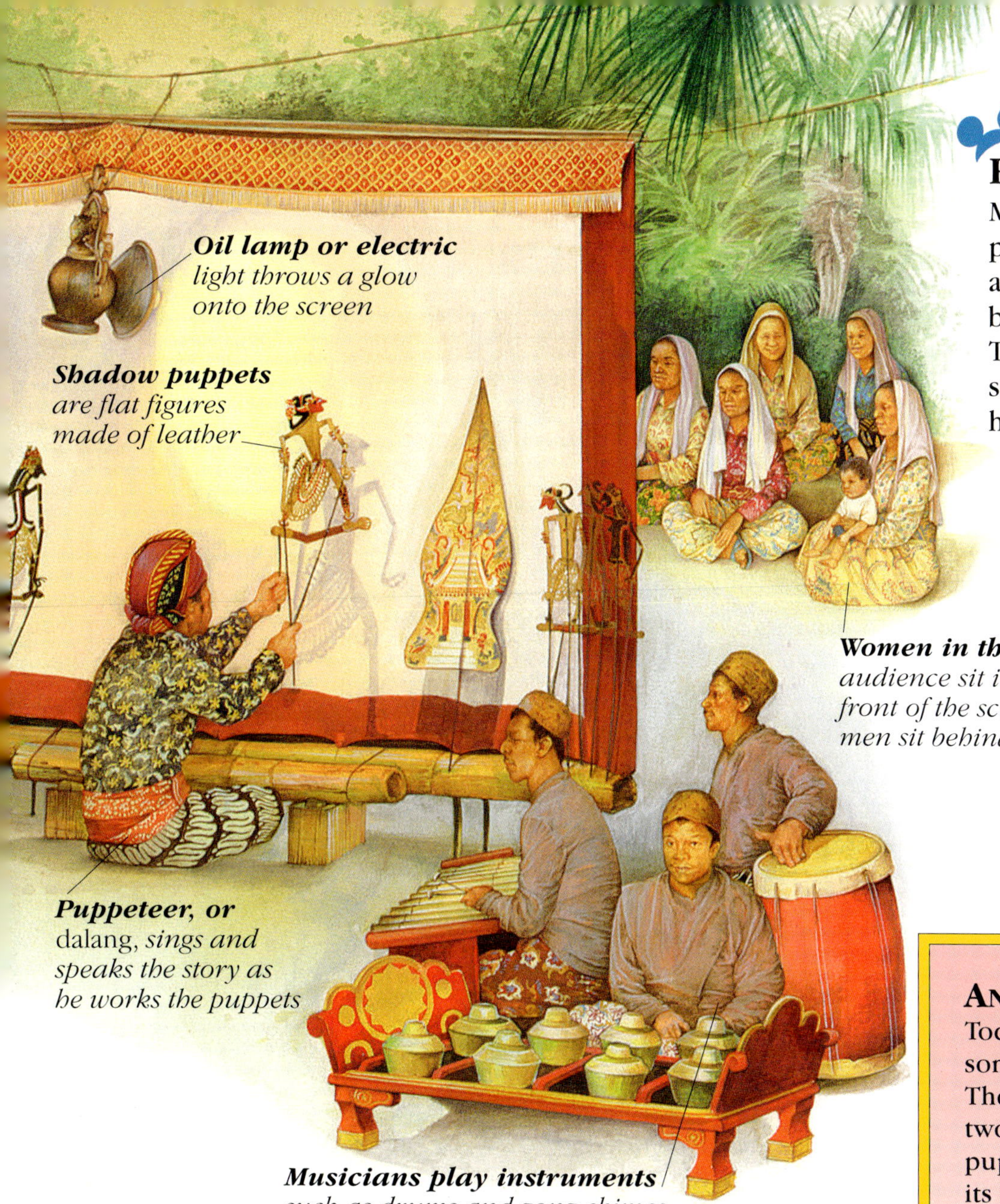

Oil lamp or electric
light throws a glow onto the screen
Shadow puppets
are flat figures made of leather
Puppeteer, or
dalang, _sings and speaks the story as he works the puppets_
Women in the
audience sit in front of the screen; men sit behind it
Musicians play instruments
such as drums and gong chimes

PUNCH AND JUDY

Mr. Punch is a famous glove puppet from England. He first appeared in the late 1600s and became popular in street shows. The shows are performed in a small tent with the puppeteer hidden from the audience.

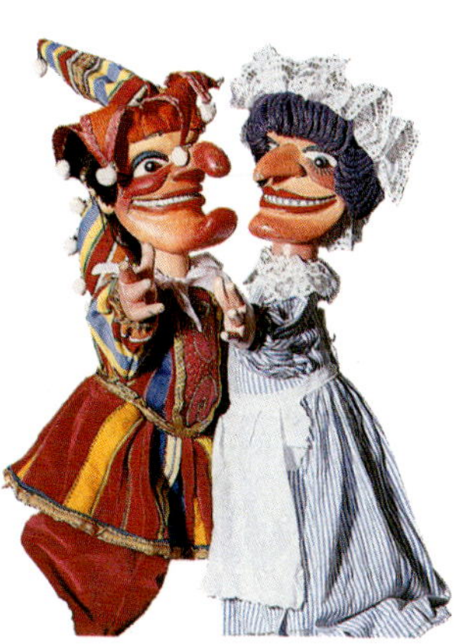

Mr. Punch with his wife, Judy

ANIMATRONICS

Today, life-sized puppets are sometimes used in the movies. These puppets are operated by two people. An actor wears the puppet's costume and controls its body movements. The facial expressions are worked by a puppeteer with radio controls.

Radio controls move the puppet's electronic face
Lifelike fur or flesh covers the electronics

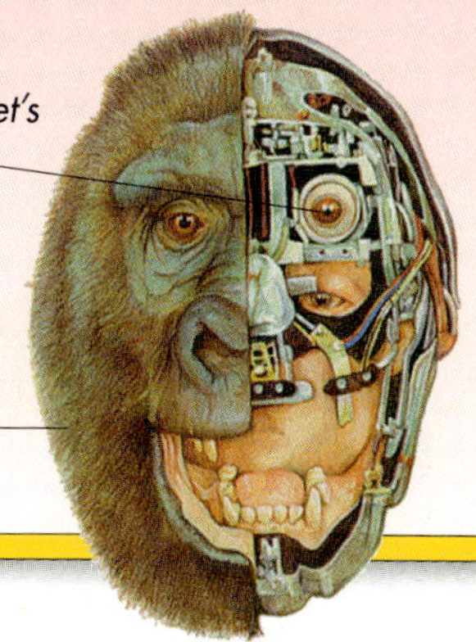

JAPANESE PUPPETS

A Bunraku puppet from Japan can make so many movements that it needs three puppeteers to work it. The puppeteers wear black and sit in full view of the audience. The chief puppeteer controls the head and the right arm. Chanters sing and speak the words.

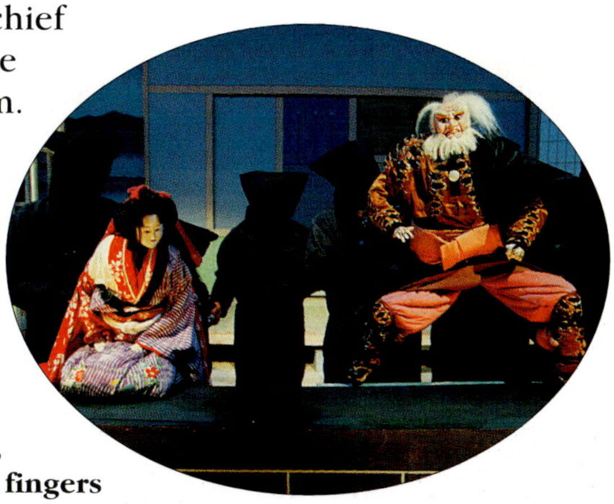

Bunraku puppets have movable eyes, mouth, hands, and fingers

FIND OUT MORE
COMMUNICATIONS: Radio waves
SCIENCE ALL AROUND US: Shadows

Plays of Ancient Greece

The Ancient Greeks, who lived about 2,500 years ago, wrote exciting plays. Thousands of people went to the amphitheaters to see these plays, and prizes were awarded for the best ones. Greek playwrights were the first to create characters who talked to each other. As well as the main actors, there was the chorus – a group of performers who sang, danced, and commented on what was happening in the play.

AMAZING FACTS

★ **The Greeks used special effects in their plays. Actors playing gods would descend on stage on a special crane.**

TRAGIC AND COMIC PLAYS

There were two main types of Greek plays: tragedy and comedy. Most Greek tragedies were based on legends. They often made the audience feel terror, horror, and pity. Comedies were funny and rude, and often poked fun at famous people.

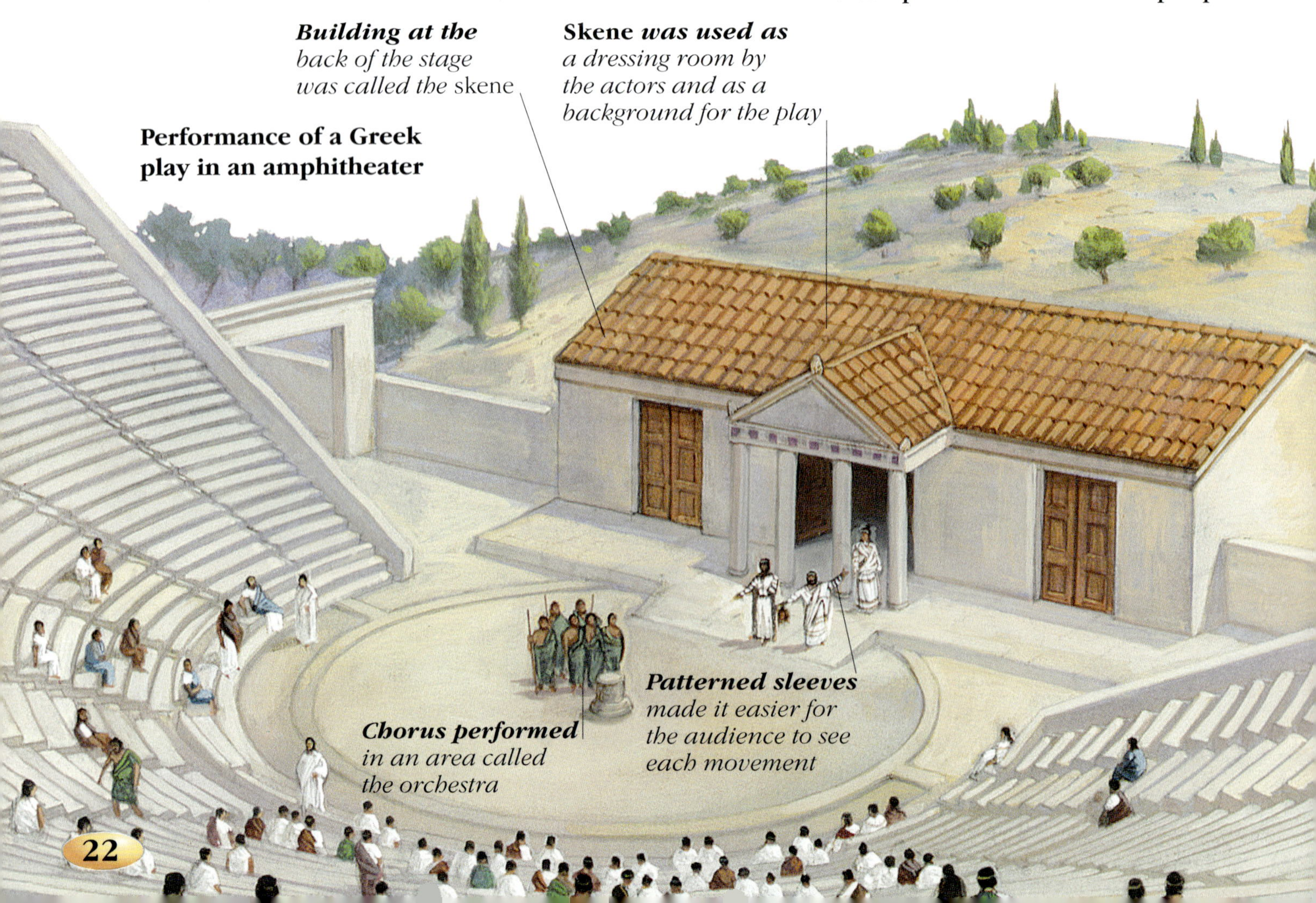

Performance of a Greek play in an amphitheater

GREEK THEATERS

The first permanent Greek theaters were built about 2,300 years ago. They were made without roofs, in the shape of a semicircle, and had rows of steeply sloping seats for the audience. The Greeks called these theaters amphitheaters. The ruins of some amphitheaters can still be seen today.

Amphitheater in the Ancient Greek city at Ephesus, Turkey

GRUESOME GAMES

The Romans built theaters that were like two Greek theaters stuck together to make a big stadium. They usually preferred to watch large spectacles, such as gladiator fights, instead of plays. Crowds of 50,000 would gather to watch these dramatic, but often violent, displays.

MASKED MEN

All the characters in Ancient Greek plays were acted by men – even the female ones. Each actor played more than one part. The actors used masks so the audience knew which character they were playing.

Mask worn by character in a comedy

Greek masks *were made of linen cloth stiffened with glue*

Mask covered *the whole head*

Seats for *the audience*

Mask worn by character in a tragedy

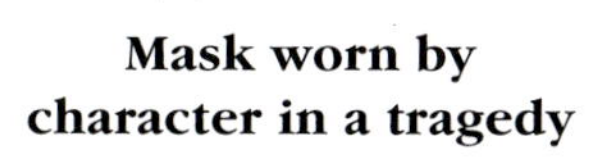

FIND OUT MORE
FAMOUS PLACES: Colosseum
STORY OF THE PAST: Mediterranean world

Shows on Wheels

In the 1400s and 1500s, many towns in Europe put on plays to celebrate Christian festivals. The plays were based on Bible stories and were performed on carts, called pageants, which were pulled around the town. Even today, street shows and colorful processions take place all around the world to celebrate many different religious festivals.

MOVING DRAMA

The actors on a pageant performed one Bible scene and moved on. Another pageant, with the actors for the next scene, then took its place. The pageant actors were often local craftsmen who staged a scene that showed off their skills.

Some people watched *from the windows of their houses*

Each pageant *was decorated for the scene that was acted on it*

Pageant for *Noah's Ark*

Machinery for *lowering actors onto the stage*

Stage machinery

MAGICAL MACHINERY

Actors in pageant plays used the space beneath the stage on their carts to hide machinery. This machinery was used for trick effects, such as lowering an actor onto the stage from above.

HUGE CROWDS

Crowds of people gathered to watch religious pageant plays in Europe. These plays were popular because the actors spoke in everyday language, not Latin, which was the language spoken in the Christian church.

Amazing Facts

★ **In 1633, many people in Oberammergau, Germany, were killed by the plague. The survivors, to give thanks, vowed to put on a religious play every 10 years – a tradition that continues to this day.**

Hundreds of people pull each float

Fantastic Floats

Nowadays, one of the biggest pageant processions takes place each July in Orissa, India. Enormous decorated floats are pulled through the streets in honor of the Hindu god Jagannatha.

Horses pulled *each pageant through the crowded streets*

People watching the Noah's Ark scene

The whole town *enjoyed the spectacle*

Carnival

Colorful parades of decorated carts, or floats, still take place around the world. For example, two months before the Christian festival of Easter, people in Brazil take to the streets in parades of singing and dancing.

Rio de Janeiro carnival, in Brazil, lasts five full days

FIND OUT MORE
CHILDREN OF THE WORLD: Carnival
COMMUNICATIONS: Spoken word

Japanese Theater

Japan is well known for two main kinds of drama – Noh and Kabuki. Noh is a serious dance-drama, performed on a traditional stage without much scenery. It began in the 1300s and was first acted by priests from Buddhist temples. Today it is performed by ordinary actors. Kabuki began in the early 1600s. It is much livelier than Noh, with songs, dance, funny scenes, energetic fights, and splendid scenery.

Poetry in Motion

Noh plays are always performed on a special stage, which has two acting areas – a main stage and a bridge that links the main stage to the mirror room. Many Noh plays tell Buddhist stories. They are told partly in poetry, which is sung by the performers.

Painted pine tree *is a reminder of when the plays were performed outdoors*

Mirror room where *actors check their costumes before going on stage*

Bridge joins *the mirror room to the main stage*

Trees set in *pebbles are the only decoration*

Traditional Noh theater

Kabuki *Mie*

When a Kabuki play reaches an exciting moment, the male characters "freeze" to hold an eye-catching pose. This is called *mie* and draws attention to what the character is feeling at this important turning point in the story.

Actor is playing *a proud lion*

Kabuki actor

Props

Both Noh and Kabuki use few props. But they make clever use of the ones they do have. In Kabuki, a fan can represent a number of different things, such as a sword, chopsticks, or falling leaves.

Colorful Kabuki fan

Simple Masks

Noh performers use a grand, formal style of acting. They move slowly and precisely. The main actors usually wear simple face masks.

Noh masks are carved from wood and painted

Amazing Facts

★ Japanese theaters were the first to have stages that revolved, or turned around. The revolving part was turned from below by helpers called stagehands.

FIND OUT MORE
PAINTING AND SCULPTURE:
Fans, Japanese prints

Elizabethan Theater

William Shakespeare

In 1576, during the reign of Queen Elizabeth I, a huge wooden theater was built in London, England. It was built as a circle so that people could sit most of the way around the stage. The theater was so successful that others like it were built nearby. One of these theaters, called the Globe, put on the plays of the great English playwright William Shakespeare. He wrote 37 plays about everything from murder and war, to love and jealousy.

POPULAR PLAYWRIGHT

William Shakespeare lived from 1564 to 1616. He was an actor and poet as well as a playwright. He usually wrote in poetry, or verse. Some of his characters make long solo speeches, called soliloquies, that tell the audience about their inner thoughts.

Hamlet (left) fighting his rival, Laertes

ACTION PLAYS

Shakespeare's plays are full of action and excitement. For example, in his play *Hamlet*, the hero meets a ghost, survives a pirate attack, commits a murder, and then fights a thrilling sword fight against his opponent, Laertes, who has a poisoned sword.

PERFORMING SHAKESPEARE

Shakespeare's plays have been translated into many languages and performed all over the world. Some have been made into films, and others have been made into musicals and operas.

Scene from a film version of *Henry V*

Stage

Actors

Performance at the Globe theater

People in the standing audience were called groundlings – they were often noisy

The Globe

Many of Shakespeare's plays were performed at the Globe. This theater could hold an audience of about 3,000. People who could afford seats sat around the sides of the theater. Those with less money stood around the stage.

Amazing Facts

★ In 1613, a spark from a cannon set fire to the thatch roof of the Globe, burning down the theater in two hours.

Modern-day Globe

In 1997, a new Globe theater was opened in London. It was built in the style of the original Globe, using the same materials and building methods. Audiences in Shakespeare's day often threw food at characters they did not like, but today's audiences are usually well behaved.

Aerial view of the rebuilt Globe

FIND OUT MORE
GREAT LIVES: William Shakespeare
SPORT: Fencing

Indoor Stages

The first permanent indoor theaters were built in Italy in the late 1500s. For the first time, complicated scenery could be used and changed between scenes. Early indoor theaters had a frame around the stage. The frame made the scenery look as if it was inside a picture frame. There are still picture-frame theaters today, but new theaters often have stages that can be changed to suit each play.

AMAZING FACTS

★ Before the days of electric lights, many theaters burned down after candle flames set fire to the scenery.

PRETTY AS A PICTURE

Early picture-frame stages were lit by candles hanging in chandeliers or placed along the front of the stage. The stage sloped upward slightly toward the back, to give more of a sense of distance.

Picture frame *is also called a proscenium arch*

Curtain is drawn *when the scenery needs to be changed*

Boxes at the side *of the stage are for wealthier members of the audience*

Picture-frame stage

Lights at the front *of the stage are called footlights*

Audience *sits in rows*

Painted *scenery*

ALL AROUND THE STAGE

A theater where the audience sits all around the acting area is called a theater in the round. This kind of staging is popular today, but it is not a modern invention – Roman amphitheaters were very similar.

Actors on stage in a theater in the round

MODERN THEATER BUILDINGS

Brand-new theater buildings often contain two or more different stages. This means that several different plays can be performed at the same time. A building with several theaters in it is called a theater complex.

London's modern Royal National Theatre contains three different stages

GETTING CLOSER

Stages that do not have a frame and are open to an audience on three sides are called open stages. They bring the actors and audience much closer together.

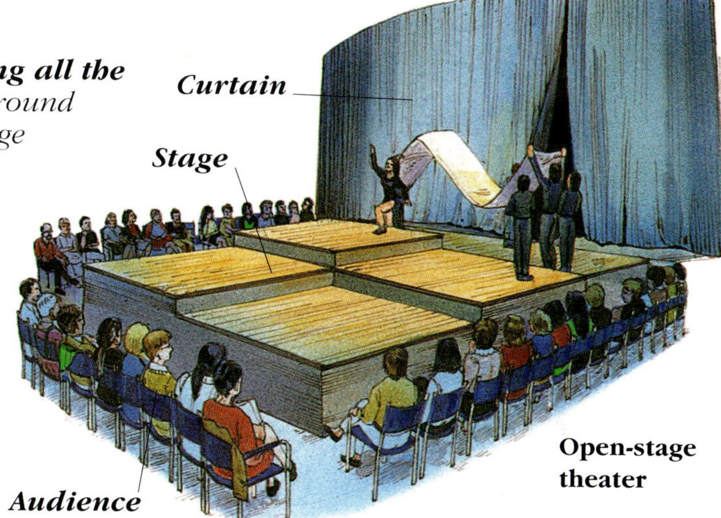

Open-stage theater

CHANGING SCENERY

The introduction of indoor theaters meant there was somewhere permanent to make and store scenery. As scenery became more elaborate, scenes were painted onto a cloth that hung at the back of the stage or onto thin cut-outs of wood.

Stagehands changing scenery

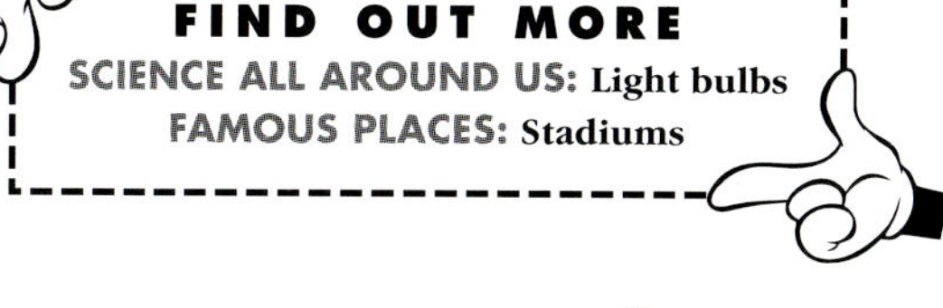

FIND OUT MORE
SCIENCE ALL AROUND US: **Light bulbs**
FAMOUS PLACES: **Stadiums**

All the Fun of the Circus

A circus is a spectacular traveling show of strong men, acrobats, clowns, musicians, and many other performers. Both Russia and China have famous state circuses that have performed around the world.

The first true circuses began in the late 1700s in England. They included daring horse-riding displays and clowning. Other acts were added, such as juggling, acrobatics, lion taming, and wild animal displays. Many circus shows took place inside huge tents. Today, many people do not like to see animals perform, so some circuses do not include animals.

Juggling, like other circus skills, takes a lot of practice

Trapeze artists have *to time their twists and spins perfectly*

Performers and audience at a traditional circus

Circus acrobats *must have a good sense of balance*

IN THE RING

The circus ring is like the theater stage – where all the action happens. The normal size of a European circus ring is at least 13 m (43 ft) across, which is large enough to allow a horse to gallop around it comfortably.

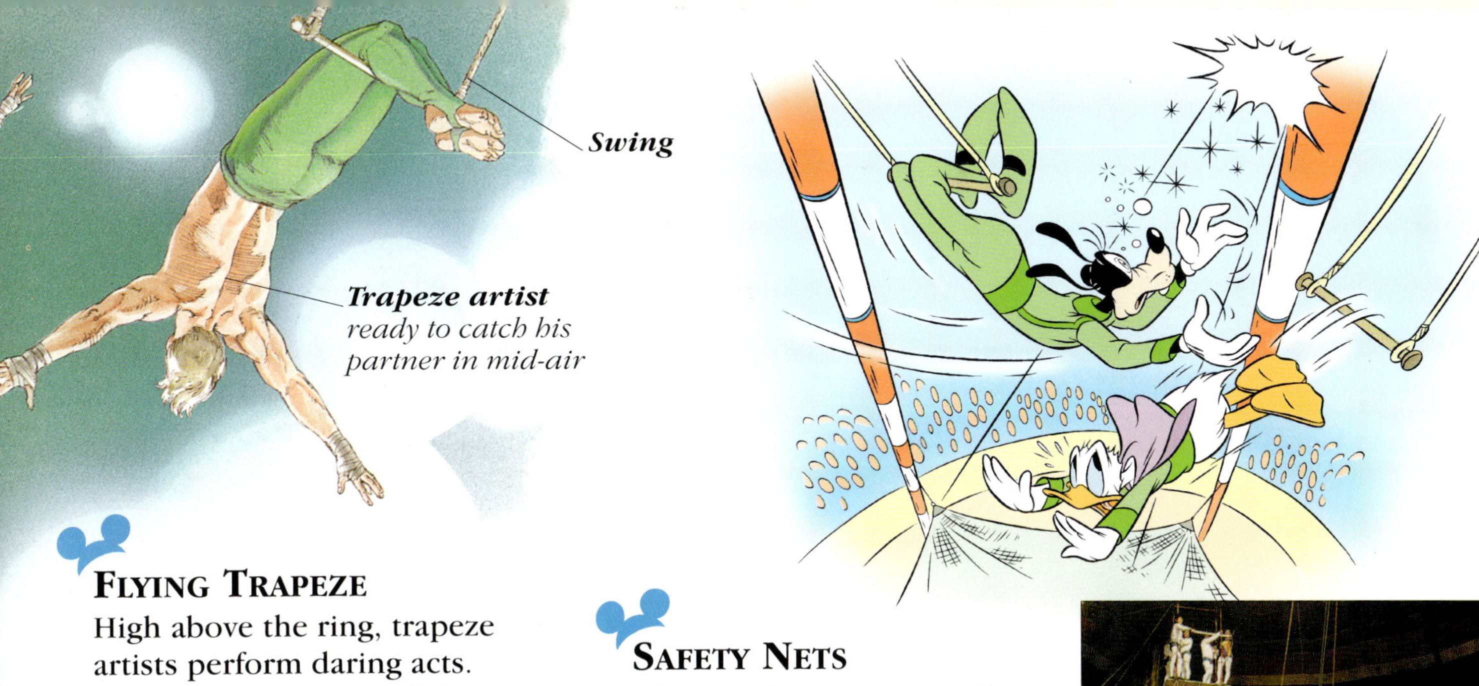

Flying Trapeze

High above the ring, trapeze artists perform daring acts. They use swings to build up speed, then let go and fly through the air to another swing or the arms of a partner who is waiting to catch them.

Safety Nets

A huge safety net is usually stretched across the ring during acrobatic acts such as the flying trapeze. It will catch performers if they fall.

Acrobatic acts are daring, but the net is there to catch performers

Clowns' Make-up

Clowns are the funny people of a circus. Most of them wear thick, colorful make-up and bright baggy clothing. In Britain, clowns register their make-up pattern by copying it onto an egg. No one else can use the same patterns and colors.

Clowns' make-up painted on eggs

Master of the Circus

The ringmaster is the person in charge of a traditional circus. The ringmaster introduces each act and keeps an eye on the clowns to make sure they behave themselves.

FIND OUT MORE
SCIENCE ALL AROUND US: Gravity
SPORT: Gymnasts

Modern Plays

In the 1870s in Europe, new kinds of plays were written about everyday life and the problems people faced at that time. The actors in these plays behaved like ordinary people – this was known as the naturalistic style of acting. The scenery and costumes were made to look as real as possible. There are other modern styles of acting, but the naturalistic style is still popular for stage, television, and the movies.

KITCHEN-SINK DRAMA

In Britain in the 1950s, some playwrights started writing realistic dramas about ordinary people. These plays are known as kitchen-sink dramas because they are often set in small apartments, where people are shown doing everyday things, such as housework.

The action is *centered around ordinary people*

In the "absurd" play *Endgame*, by Samuel Beckett, two characters spend the whole play inside trash cans

THAT'S ABSURD

During the 1950s and 1960s, a few plays were written about how life can sometimes seem very confusing. These plays are full of crazy conversations and odd happenings. This type of drama is known as theater of the absurd.

Scene is set in *the living room of a small apartment*

Scene from a kitchen-sink drama

Amazing Facts

★ **Most modern plays last two or three hours. But Robert Wilson's play *Overture to Ka Mountain* lasted a whole week. It was performed on a mountain in Iran in 1972.**

Actors rehearsing their actions and lines

Learning Lines

Before a play is performed in front of an audience, the actors spend time learning their words and rehearsing. But sometimes actors forget their words. A person called a prompt follows the play from off stage and calls out the words to the actor.

Scenery includes *real furniture*

Television Drama

Popular television shows about everyday life are called soap operas. They are usually about the relationships in a family or a group of friends and are often quite sentimental. Other television dramas include more action, such as exciting car chases.

Scene from *NYPD Blue*, an American drama set in the New York police department

FIND OUT MORE
COMMUNICATIONS: Television
GREAT LIVES: Film stars

Operas and Musicals

An opera is a play in which the words are sung to music played by an orchestra. The main characters sing to tell the audience about the story and about their feelings. There is usually a chorus, too. Opera began in Italy in the early 1600s. In a musical, song is mixed with both speech and dance. Musicals became popular in the United States at the start of the 1900s.

HIGH AND LOW

Women have higher singing voices than men. A male singer can be a bass, baritone, or tenor. A woman can have a contralto, mezzo-soprano, or soprano voice. Bass is the lowest singing voice and soprano is the highest.

The part of the hero *is often sung by a tenor*

Tenor and soprano singing a duet

The Opera House in Paris, France

SPECIAL THEATERS

Operas are performed in an opera house. Inside, the musicians sit in an area called the orchestra pit below and in front of the stage.

Move those Feet

Tap dancing is often used in musicals. The dancers wear shoes that have pieces of metal fixed to the toes and heels. They move their feet so the metal makes a rhythmic tapping sound.

Early tap shoes were wooden, but after about 1925 metal plates (left) were used

Dance routine in a musical

Showtime

Modern musicals are often spectacular to watch. They have catchy tunes, energetic dancing, brilliant lighting effects, and amazing scenery.

Scene from the modern musical *Miss Saigon*

Musicals and Dancing

The music and songs for a musical are usually more lighthearted than the music for an opera. Most musicals include fantastic dance routines, such as those in *Cats* and *Starlight Express* by Andrew Lloyd Webber. Musicals can be seen on stage or at the movies.

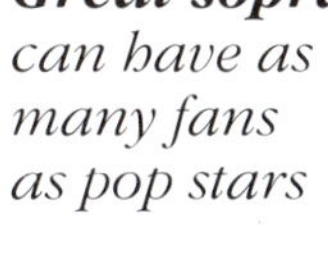

Great sopranos *can have as many fans as pop stars*

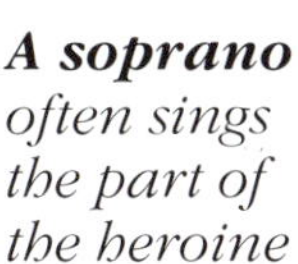

A soprano *often sings the part of the heroine*

Singers wear *costumes to suit the part they play*

Amazing Facts

★ **In 1988 an Italian opera singer called Luciano Pavarotti was applauded for over one hour by an audience after singing in an opera in Germany.**

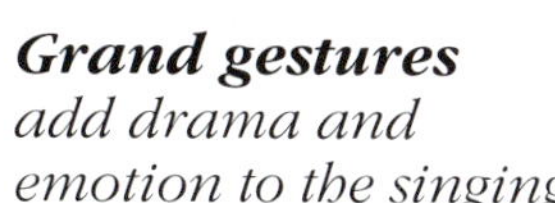

Grand gestures *add drama and emotion to the singing*

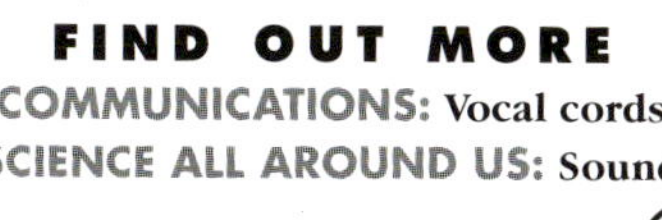

FIND OUT MORE
COMMUNICATIONS: Vocal cords
SCIENCE ALL AROUND US: Sound

Beijing Opera

Beijing opera, known as *jing xi* in China, has been performed for about 200 years. It uses a mixture of music, song, speech, mime, and acrobatics. Clever use is made of a few pieces of scenery and objects called props. For example, a banner carried on stage by a single soldier can represent a whole army.

There is little
fixed scenery
Actors wearing
colorful costumes
Heroine is
played by
a male actor

Traditional characters in a Beijing opera

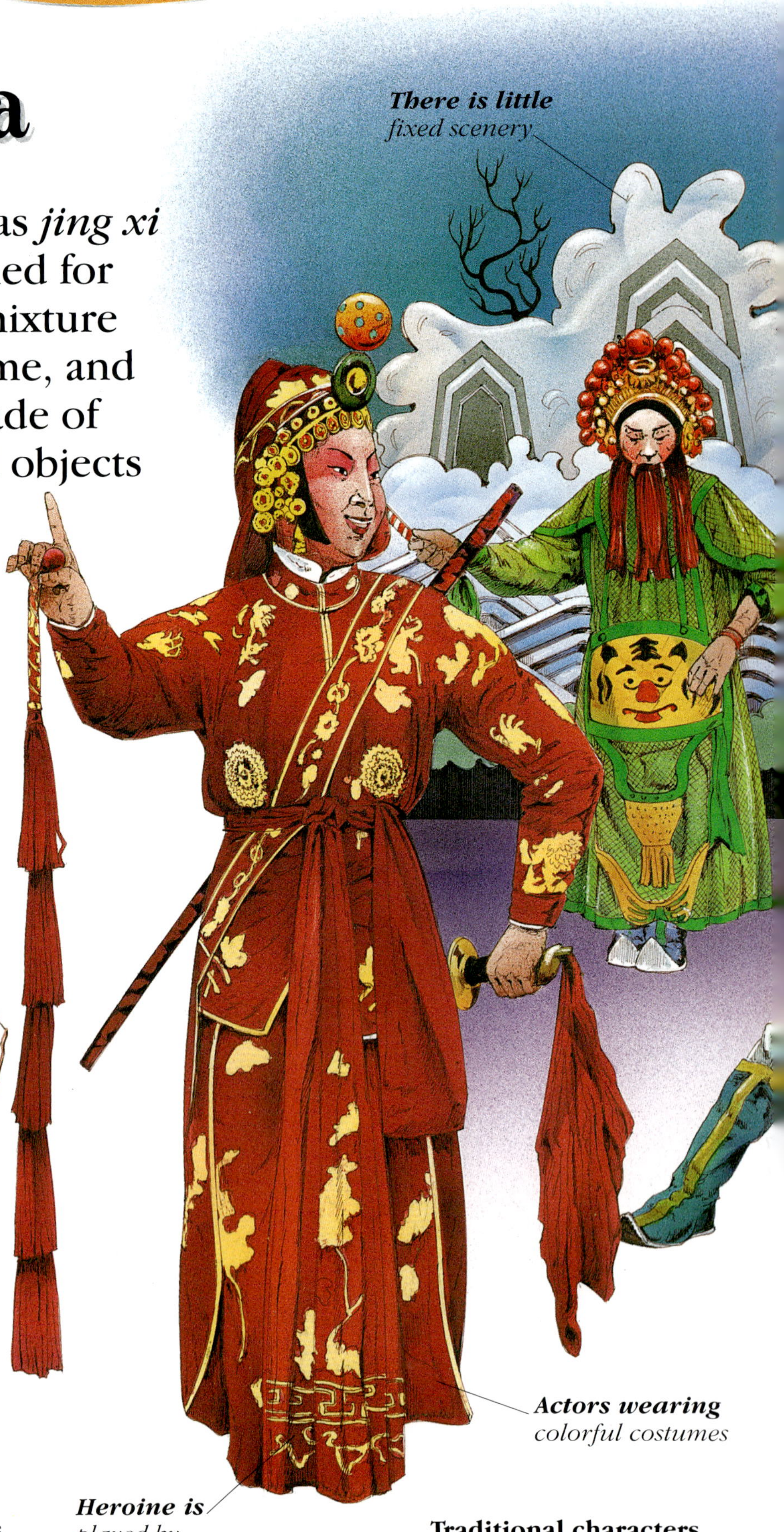

STORIES FROM THE PAST

Many Beijing operas are based on historical stories and romantic books of China's past. One of the most popular operas, *Beauty*, tells the true tale of a kidnapped princess who dies for her country.

Wooden clappers
Gong
Huqin

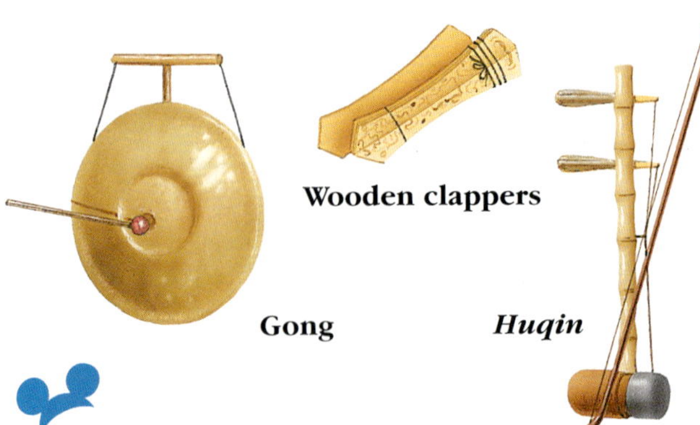

OPERA INSTRUMENTS

A cymbal and gong are played at the start of each performance and also when an actor enters or leaves the stage. Other instruments used include wooden clappers and the *huqin,* a two-stringed fiddle.

AMAZING FACTS

★ **About 1,800 years ago, Chinese warriors painted their faces with bright colors to terrify their enemies. This is the origin of Chinese theater make-up.**

MAKE-UP LIKE A MASK

A character's make-up shows what that character is like. A red face is loyal and brave, a white face is cunning and deceitful, and a dark face is strong and rough. A gold face is worn by gods and goddesses.

Mask worn by a strong character

Gold coloring for a god or goddess

BATTLE ACROBATS

Beijing opera often includes acrobatic fight scenes. In dazzling displays, the actors somersault, cartwheel, and throw and catch weapons to the sounds of gongs and cymbals.

Acrobatic movements *are often used to show fighting*

Acrobatic actors leaping and jumping

VOICE TRAINING

Stage actors and singers have to learn to project, or "throw," their voices, so that they can be heard clearly without having to strain and shout. They spend a lot of time doing special exercises to train their voices.

Voice training is essential for a good performance

FIND OUT MORE
CHILDREN OF THE WORLD: China
COMMUNICATIONS: Cymbal

Special Effects

Stage tricks, such as a ghost appearing on stage, are called special effects. They are created by machinery and lighting equipment that the audience cannot see.

Make-up can also be used to create fantastic effects. An actor's teeth can be painted with black tooth paint to make them look as though they have fallen out. Realistic scars can be made from a rubbery material called latex. The scars are stuck onto the skin with a glue called spirit gum.

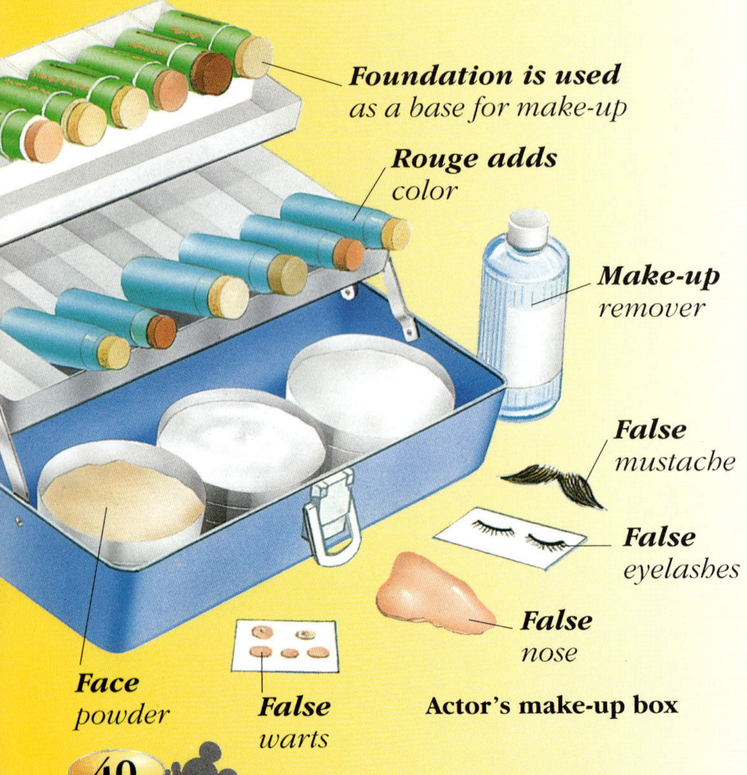
Foundation is used *as a base for make-up*

Rouge adds *color*

Make-up *remover*

False *mustache*

False *eyelashes*

False *nose*

Face *powder*

False *warts*

Actor's make-up box

FLYING ON STAGE

For an actor to "fly" magically across a stage, he or she must put on a harness underneath the costume. The harness is then attached to machinery above the stage by a long wire. When the wire is pulled, the actor flies through the air.

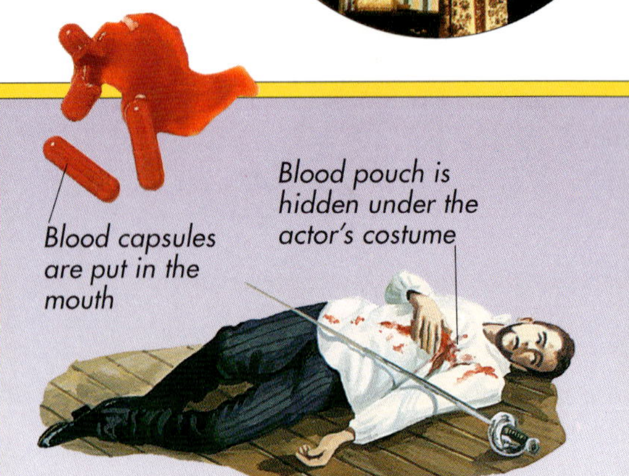
Wire and harness cannot be seen by the audience

Blood capsules are put in the mouth

Blood pouch is hidden under the actor's costume

PRETEND BLOOD

Fake blood is stored in capsules or thin plastic pouches. Actors burst these capsules and pouches when they pretend to die or be injured.

Trick Trap

A trapdoor is a small part of a stage floor that can be lifted or lowered by machinery underneath the stage. Actors sometimes use trapdoors to appear from beneath the stage or to disappear down underneath it.

Colored smoke *gives a mysterious effect*

Actor being raised through a trapdoor

Stagehand *operates the trapdoor and lift from below*

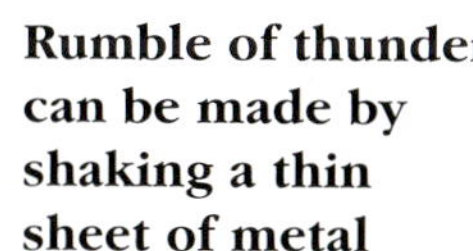

Rumble of thunder can be made by shaking a thin sheet of metal

Shaking and rattling dried peas can sound like rain or the sea

Sound Effects

Behind the scenes, stagehands operate sound effects, such as the crash of waves or the clip-clop of horses' hooves. Sounds can be created by hand or played as tape recordings.

Stage lights are controlled from the lighting desk

Stage Lighting

Modern indoor theaters have rows of powerful electric lights that are hung high above the stage. An operator sits at a control system above and behind the audience to work these lights.

FIND OUT MORE
GREAT INVENTIONS: Recording
INSIDE MACHINES: Pulleys

Ingredients of Music

Sounds are vibrations, or tiny shaking movements, in the air. Your ears pick up the vibrations and your brain then tells you what the sound is. The pitch of a sound is how high or low the sound is. Music is made up of sounds called notes, and a melody, or tune, is a collection of different notes arranged into a pattern. Harmony is a lovely sound created by playing or singing two or more notes together.

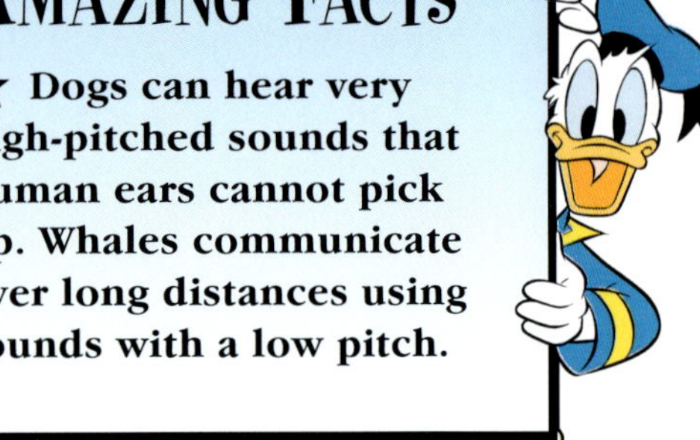

AMAZING FACTS

★ **Dogs can hear very high-pitched sounds that human ears cannot pick up. Whales communicate over long distances using sounds with a low pitch.**

WRITTEN MUSIC

A composer is someone who creates music. Most composers write their music down so other musicians can play the piece in exactly the way the composer wants it.

Time signature *describes the beat that runs through a piece of music*

The sign mf tells *you to play the music moderately loud*

Musical notes are *written on a set of five lines called a staff*

Treble clef tells *you to play these notes with your right hand*

Bass clef tells *you to play these notes with your left hand*

Piece of music written down for the piano

The seven notes in a Western scale are named with letters from the alphabet

MUSICAL SCALE

A scale is a pattern of notes, each with a different pitch. Different scales are used around the world. In China and Africa, many scales have five notes. In Western music, scales usually have seven different notes.

Choirs usually sing in harmony

SINGING IN HARMONY

A choir is a group of people who sing together. The singers are often divided into groups. Each group sings different notes to create beautiful harmonies.

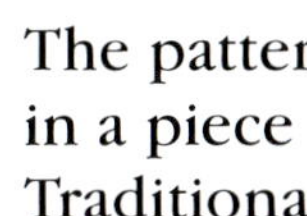

RHYTHM

The patterns of long and short sounds in a piece of music are called rhythms. Traditional African music has exciting rhythms that are made with hand claps, drums, and rattles.

Clapping in time to the music is an easy way to hear the rhythm of a piece

Metronome produces a steady ticking sound to tell musicians how fast the beat should be

Each time of day has a different raga

RAGAS

Indian scales are made up of notes arranged in patterns called ragas. Each raga creates a different mood or feeling and should be played at a particular time of day or year.

FIND OUT MORE
COMMUNICATIONS: Writing
HUMAN BODY: Feelings

Wind Instruments

Some musical instruments make a sound when a player blows into them. They are called wind instruments. When the player blows, the air inside the tube vibrates and gives out a note. Different notes are made by changing the length of the vibrating column of air inside the tube. This is done by covering and uncovering holes with the fingers, by pressing keys or valves, or, as with a trombone, by moving a sliding part.

SQUEEZE BAG

Bagpipes are made up of pipes attached to a bag. The bagpipe player blows into the bag until it is full of air. The air is then squeezed out through the pipes. As the vibrating air flows through the pipes, it makes sounds.

Scottish bagpipe player

Air flows *through pipes*

Bag fills with *air as the piper blows*

Pipe with *fingerholes to change pitch of notes*

Movable slide *changes the length of the trombone tube*

Tubas are *heavy to carry*

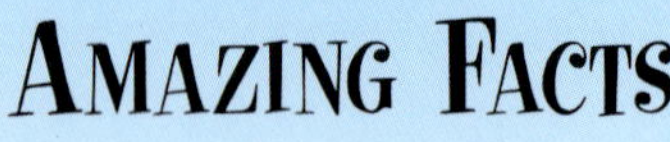

AMAZING FACTS

★ **The oldest flutes known are bones with holes in them. They are over 20,000 years old.**

★ **In ancient times conch sea shells were used as trumpets on many islands in the Pacific Ocean.**

PLAYING AND WALKING

A marching band has different types of wind instruments. Brass instruments, such as the tuba, are made of metal. Like the trumpet, the tuba has buttons called valves. When pressed, these valves open or close different lengths of tube.

Pan pipes are made up of tubes of different lengths

Nose flute player from Indonesia

Ancient Pipes

The gentle, breathy-sounding pan pipes have been played in Peru, Bolivia, and other parts of South America for thousands of years. Each tube in a set of pan pipes sounds a different note.

Tube of a *French horn forms a loop*

Cornets are *like small trumpets*

Marching brass band

Nose Flute

Some flutes are played with air blown from the nose instead of through the mouth. Nose flutes are played on many Pacific islands and by the people who live in the Amazon rain forest.

Little and Large

The piccolo measures just 32 cm (12½ in), while the largest tuba ever made stands at 2.28 m (7½ ft) tall.

FIND OUT MORE
INSIDE MACHINES: Valves
SCIENCE ALL AROUND US: Sound

Strings, Percussion, and Keyboard

String instruments have tightly stretched strings that vibrate to make sound. To play different notes, the player presses down on the strings with the fingers of one hand. With the other hand, the player plucks the strings or strokes them with a stick called a bow. Instruments that you hit, shake, or scrape are called percussion instruments. Keyboard instruments have keys that you press down to play the different notes.

AMAZING FACTS

★ In October 1979, four Japanese string musicians put on diving masks and played their instruments under water. They could hear each other because sound travels through water as well as air.

***Sitar player** sits down to play*

***When the strings** vibrate, the air in the hollow body of the sitar vibrates too, making the sound louder*

Playing the Indian sitar

SHIMMERING SITAR

The sitar is an important instrument in classical Indian music. When the player plucks the main strings, a second set of strings also vibrates, making a shimmering sound.

VIOLIN

Like many stringed instruments, the violin is played with a bow. A bow is a rod of wood with horsehair stretched tightly between its ends.

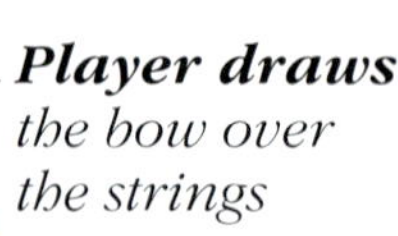

***Violin is** held under the chin*

***Player draws** the bow over the strings*

Playing the violin

All Kinds of Percussion

There are hundreds of different percussion instruments. On some, such as the xylophone, players can play tunes because the notes have exact pitches. Others, such as maracas, do not have any particular pitch.

Bongo drums are hit with the hands

Maracas are shaken to make a sound

Each bar of a xylophone sounds a different note when it is hit

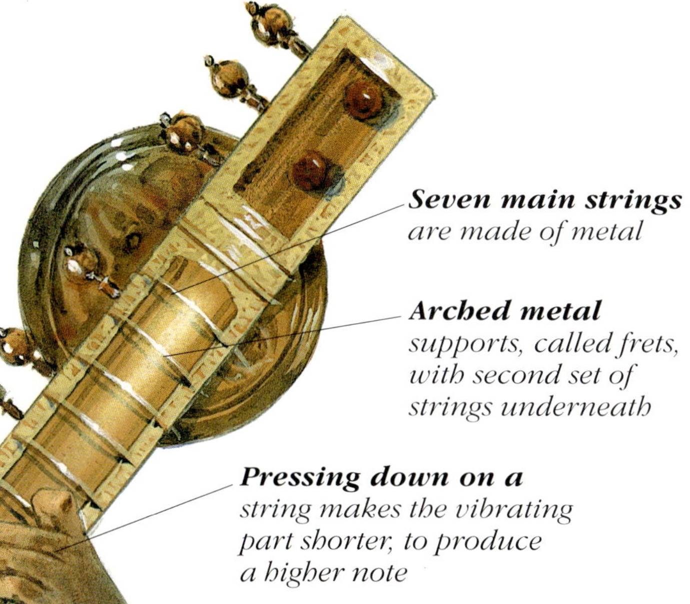

Seven main strings *are made of metal*

Arched metal *supports, called frets, with second set of strings underneath*

Pressing down on a *string makes the vibrating part shorter, to produce a higher note*

How a Piano Key Works

Inside a piano there are lots of tightly stretched strings. When you press a key on the piano's keyboard, a hammer lifts to hit a string. When you let go of the key, a block of felt, called a damper, drops to stop the string from vibrating.

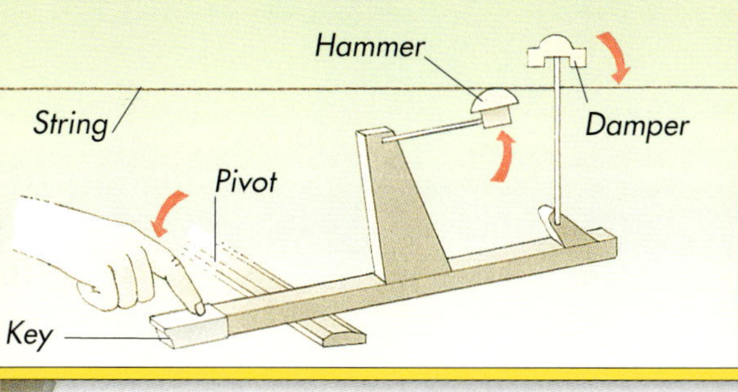

Concert Pianos

Pianists often perform to audiences in huge halls called concert halls. The pianos they play are called grand pianos and have their strings laid out flat. Upright pianos are smaller. Their strings run vertically behind the keys.

Top of the grand piano is opened to let out more of the sound

FIND OUT MORE
GREAT LIVES: Yehudi Menuhin
SCIENCE ALL AROUND US: Sound

Electric and Electronic Music

Electric and electronic instruments make their sounds with the help of electricity. An electric guitar or violin produces sounds in the usual way, but uses electricity to make them louder. An electronic keyboard has a computer memory that can store the sounds of other musical instruments. The player uses the keyboard like a piano but chooses the type of sound by pressing a button.

Electric Music

There is a microphone on an electric guitar that changes the string vibrations into electrical signals. An amplifier then makes these signals louder, and a loudspeaker changes them back into sounds.

Musicians wear *headphones so they can concentrate on the sound from their own instrument*

Musicians inside a recording studio

Knobs on the mixing *desk control the volume of each instrument*

The instruments' *sounds are mixed together on a mixing desk*

Mixing Music

Music recordings are made in a recording studio. Sound engineers usually record each instrument separately, making sure the sounds are balanced and easy to hear. They then mix them together to make a master recording that is used to make CDs and cassettes.

SAMPLING BOX

A sampler is an electronic device that records short pieces of sounds. The sounds are altered into patterns of numbers and stored electronically. They can then be changed and controlled by a person using a computer keyboard.

Modern band using a sampler

Electric guitars are *played in the same way as normal guitars*

Electric instruments *are plugged into an amplifier*

Electronic *synthesizer*

ELECTRONIC MIXER

A synthesizer is an electronic keyboard that can store any sounds and change or mix them exactly as the player wishes. It can also produce totally new electronic sounds.

Electronic synthesizer

Display panel *shows which type of sounds are selected*

Electronic drum machine

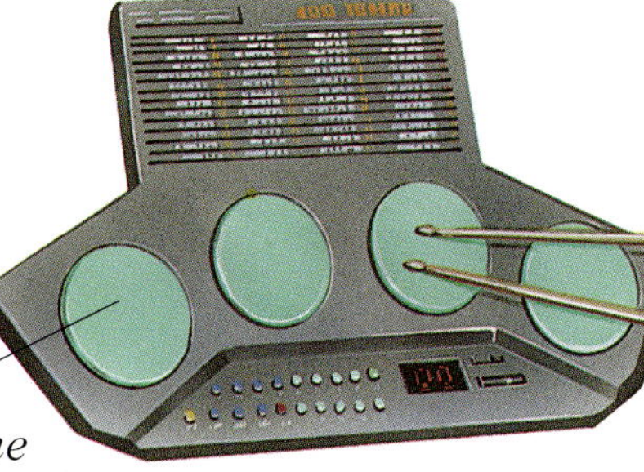

Pads on *drum machine*

DRUM BEATS

Electronic drum machines can make lots of drum sounds. Some of them have pads to play the rhythm on. Most pop recordings today use a drum machine instead of a large, full drum set.

Foot controls can *change the sound produced by the electric guitar*

AMAZING FACTS

★ In Japan there is a robot called WABOT-2, which can play a keyboard faster than a person.

FIND OUT MORE
COMMUNICATIONS: Digital sound
INSIDE MACHINES: Computers

The Orchestra

An orchestra is a large group of musicians who play a mixture of instruments together. The largest type of orchestra is called a symphony orchestra. It usually has about 80 players.

A symphony orchestra is made up of string, wind, and percussion instruments. The symphony orchestra began to develop in the 1700s, when composers started to write music especially for it. Nowadays the symphony orchestra plays all sorts of music, from classical symphonies to pop music. In Japan, *gagaku* music is played in temples and at the emperor's court. A *gagaku* orchestra has about 20 different instruments. *Gagaku* music is over 1,000 years old.

***Flutes play the tune** in* gagaku *music*

Gagaku musicians

SYMPHONY AND CONCERTO

A symphony is a piece of music that is written for all the instruments of the orchestra. The piece is usually composed in three or four different sections, called movements. In a concerto, a solo instrument, such as the piano, violin, or cello, is accompanied by the orchestra.

Vanessa Mae, a solo violinist, stands in front of the orchestra to play a concerto

Symphony orchestra

Percussion section

Harps

Violins

SYMPHONY ORCHESTRA

Most of the stringed instruments in a symphony orchestra are grouped together at the front. The noisier wind, brass, and percussion instruments are at the back. The string section is bigger than the other groups to make up for the quieter sound of its instruments.

Indonesian gamelan

Round gong *chimes are made of metal*

Gamelan Orchestra

An Indonesian orchestra is called a gamelan. It is made up of between 20 and 75 instruments including hanging gongs, metal and wooden xylophones, gong chimes, and drums.

Woodwind section

Brass section

Double basses

Violas and cellos

Conductor stands on *a raised platform so he can be easily seen*

Giving Direction

A conductor stands in front of the orchestra and signals when, how quickly, and how loudly to play. The conductor often uses a white stick called a baton.

FIND OUT MORE
GREAT LIVES: Wolfgang Amadeus Mozart
SCIENCE ALL AROUND US: Acoustics

Jazz, Swing, and Blues

In the early 1900s, a new style of music developed in North America from a mix of African and European music. It was called jazz and it quickly became popular worldwide. Jazz musicians often start with a familiar tune and then improvise, or change it, as they go along. Jazz was influenced by the slow, sad tones of blues music, which developed in the late 1800s. Swing was a new style of jazz that appeared in the 1930s.

All the instruments *can be used in exciting solo sections, called riffs*

SINGING THE BLUES

The first recordings of blues songs were made in the 1920s. A singer sang to the music of a piano or small jazz band. One of the greatest blues singers of all was Bessie Smith. She had a hard life and poured all her feelings into her singing.

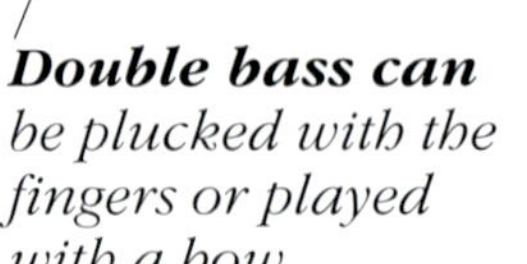

Double bass can *be plucked with the fingers or played with a bow*

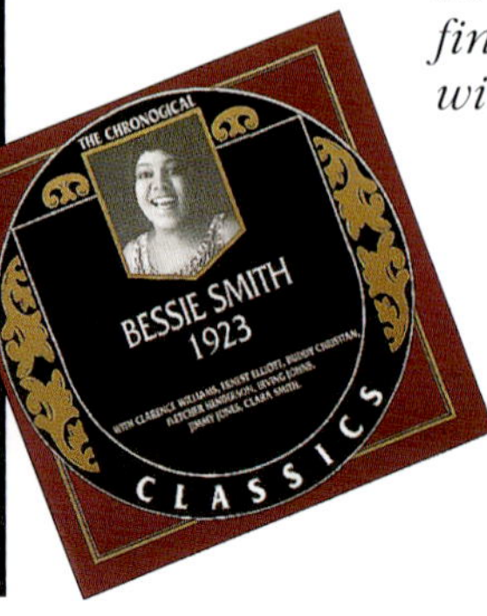

American Bessie Smith was famous for singing the blues

JAZZ BAND

Most early jazz music was created by black Americans. Jazz bands included the guitar, double bass, drums, violin, trumpet, trombone, and clarinet. Later, the banjo, piano, and saxophone also became popular.

Swing bands included trombones and saxophones

SWING

In the 1930s and 1940s, large jazz orchestras played a new kind of jazz called swing. Many people loved to dance to the lively beat of the swing bands.

AMAZING FACTS

★ Some musicians used washboards to make music. A washboard is a bumpy metal sheet on which clothes were rubbed to get them clean. Musicians scraped a metal thimble across the bumps to produce a sound.

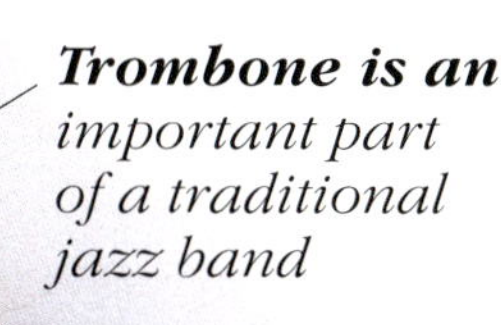

Trombone is an *important part of a traditional jazz band*

SAMBA MUSIC

Snappy Brazilian rhythms called samba have influenced musicians around the world, including American jazz musicians. Loud, lively samba music and dancing are some of the main attractions of Brazil's famous Rio carnival.

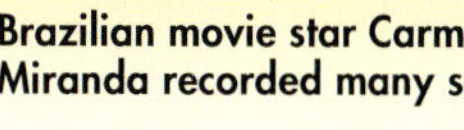

Brazilian movie star Carmen Miranda recorded many samba songs

Jazz musicians *do not usually need written music*

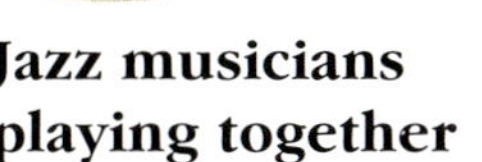

Jazz musicians playing together

FIND OUT MORE
CHILDREN OF THE WORLD:
United States of America, Carnival

Pop Music

In the 1950s, a new kind of music, called rock 'n' roll, began in North America. It was exciting, had a strong beat to dance to, and teenagers loved it. Rock 'n' roll mixed different kinds of music and usually included the sounds of electric guitars and drums. Since the 1950s, many other new styles of music have developed. All these styles together are known as pop music.

AMAZING FACTS

★ **The American pop star Michael Jackson has sold more than 47 million copies of his record *Thriller*.**

LISTENING TO ROCK 'N' ROLL

In the 1950s, many coffee shops and bars had a machine called a jukebox, which was a popular way to listen to rock 'n' roll music. Customers put a coin in a slot and chose the song they wanted to hear from the selection in the jukebox.

Most jukeboxes had a *wide choice of records*

Rock 'n' roll dancing is as lively and energetic as the music

The guitar is popular in Country and Western music

COUNTRY AND WESTERN

The music known as Country and Western began in the southern part of North America. It started as a mixture of folk songs and cowboy songs and is still popular today. It is usually played on banjos, violins, and guitars.

SHOCKING MUSIC

Punk music began in Britain in the 1970s. It was loud and angry, and the words of the songs shocked some people. Punk musicians and fans often wore ripped clothes and dyed their hair bright colors to show that they were different.

Punk singers often shouted the words to their songs

Singing Along

A karaoke machine plays songs without the voices of the singers, so that people can sing along themselves. Karaoke was invented in the 1980s in Japan. It is now popular around the world.

Karaoke performer follows the words of the song on a screen

Amplifiers make the *music loud enough for all the audience to hear*

Lots of bright lights *add atmosphere*

Playing to the Fans

Most bands like to play in front of their fans as well as making music recordings. The most famous bands tour the world to give spectacular concerts to thousands of fans.

Pop concert

Camera crew *films the concert for use in a pop video*

Audience *usually stands and dances*

Band *on stage*

FIND OUT MORE
PAINTING AND SCULPTURE: Pop art
TRAVELERS AND EXPLORERS: Bhangra

Glossary of Key Words

Actor: Someone who performs on stage, television, or in a movie.

Amphitheater: A round building with seats arranged in tiers around an open area or stage. Many were built by the Ancient Romans and Greeks and used for entertainment.

Amplifier: A machine that makes electrical signals stronger to produce louder sounds.

Animatronics: The use of electronics to make puppets move.

Characters: The people represented in a play or movie.

Choreographer: A person who plans the movements of a dance.

Chorus: The part of a song that is repeated at the end of each verse. A chorus is also a large group of people who sing together.

Classical: An art form, such as classical music or dance, that follows an established tradition.

Concert: A performance of music or dance.

Concerto: A piece of music for a solo, or single, instrument accompanied by an orchestra.

Costume: The clothes worn by a performer on stage.

Drama: A play performed on the radio, television, or at the theater.

Festival: A particular day or days that celebrate an important event or time of year with special ceremonies, dances, or meals.

Folk dance: A traditional dance.

Gestures: Movements of the hands, head, or other parts of the body that communicate a message or emotion.

Harmony: A group of notes that are played or sung together to produce a beautiful sound.

Influence: To change or to help form something. The mournful sound of blues music, for example, helped to influence the melodies and rhythms of jazz.

Key: A lever or bar on a musical instrument that is pressed down by a finger to create a note.

Keyboard: The set of keys on a piano or electrical synthesizer.

Melody: A number of different notes that are played or sung to create a tune or song.

Metronome: An instrument that, by making a regular sound, helps a musician to play in time.

Microphone: A device that turns sound into electrical signals.

Musical: A normally lighthearted play or film that includes music, singing, and dancing.

Note: A musical sound made by a voice or an instrument. A note is also the written sign that stands for a musical sound.

Opera: A play in which the words are sung to music.

Orchestra: A large group of musicians who play a variety of instruments together. Their playing is usually directed by a conductor.

Percussion: Instruments that are played by being struck, rubbed, or shaken.

Performer: Someone who entertains people by playing music, singing, dancing, or acting.

Pitch: The pitch of a sound describes how high or low it is.

Play: A story that is acted out, often on a stage.

Playwright: A writer of plays.

Poses: The positions in which an actor or dancer holds his or her body.

Procession: A line of people, or decorated carts or floats, that moves slowly along as part of a ceremony.

Prop: Something that is used by an actor in a play, such as a sword, a fan, or a piece of furniture.

Puppeteer: Someone who works with puppets, making them move in a lifelike way.

Rehearse: To practice something, such as a play or a dance, which will later be performed in public.

Rhythm: The pattern of long and short sounds in a piece of music or in a percussive beat.

Scene: A division, or part, of a play or movie that deals with a particular event.

Scenery: A backdrop that shows where a scene is taking place.

Solo: A dance, role, or musical piece performed by one person.

Spectacle: A show that is usually impressive and on a large scale.

Stage: An area in a theater where actors, dancers, or musicians perform.

Symphony: A piece of music written for an orchestra.

Synthesizer: An electronic musical instrument that can produce a wide range of different sounds.

Theater: A building where plays, ballets, and concerts are performed.

Vibration: A rapid to-and-fro movement.

Index

(*see* **Famous Places** for a full index to your complete set of books)